Original title:

Luminous Threads Over the Unicorn Yolk

Author: Aron Pilviste

ISBN HARDBACK: 978-1-80563-384-6

ISBN PAPERBACK: 978-1-80564-905-2

Enveloping Glow of Starry Nights

In the hush of night, stars gleam bright,
Whispers of secrets in the moonlight,
Each twinkle a tale, each glimmer a song,
Casting a spell, where dreamers belong.

Clouds drift softly, like thoughts in flight,
Embracing the stillness, guiding the light,
Together they dance, in the vast expanse,
Inviting the heart to a magical trance.

Crickets are singing their lullabies sweet,
Nature's soft chorus, a rhythmic beat,
Beneath the vast sky, we lay intertwined,
Lost in the wonders, our spirits aligned.

The night softly hums, a forgotten lore,
Mysteries waiting, just outside the door,
Adventure awaits in the calm of the night,
In the enveloping glow, everything feels right.

Here in this moment, we pause and we breathe,
The universe holds us, a moment to weave,
Dreams on the cusp of a beautiful flight,
Under the enchanting, starry delight.

Celestial Dreamweavers in Twilight Hues

As twilight descends, colors bleed and blend,
Waves of soft amber, the day's gentle end,
Stars begin to flicker, weaving hope in the skies,
A tapestry of dreams, where our spirit flies.

Whispers of dusk in the cool evening air,
Each breath a promise, a love laid bare,
Celestial dreamweavers, stitch the night tight,
With threads spun from laughter and silences bright.

Shadows lengthen softly, in this sacred dance,
Every heartbeat pulses, in a trance-like chance,
The moon's silver glow, a guardian near,
Illuminating paths, whispering: 'No fear.'

Lost in the twilight, where wishes collide,
Stars twinkle knowingly, our dreams as our guide,
Through realms of enchantment, we wander and roam,
Celestial guardians, forever our home.

So with hearts wide open, we embrace the night,
In celestial harmony, our souls take flight,
Together we revel in silence and song,
As dreamweavers gather, where we all belong.

Mystical Patterns Beneath the Moon's Gaze

In shadows deep where secrets lie,
The moon unfolds her silver sigh.
Whispers swirl in night's embrace,
As dreams take flight in a timeless space.

Stars twinkle bright in velvet skies,
Casting spells with ancient ties.
Patterns dance on the forest floor,
Mysteries beckon, forevermore.

The cool breeze hums a gentle tune,
While magic weaves beneath the moon.
In every leaf, in every stone,
Lies a tale of the unknown.

Time drifts slow like a sleepy tide,
In this world where dreams abide.
Every heart holds a wish or two,
Beneath the moon, forever true.

So pause and look, let your heart soar,
For life's great wonders are at your door.
In the twilight's kiss, find your way,
As mystical patterns gently play.

Sparkling Echoes of a Celestial Dance

In the silence, stars do sway,
Dancing light in a cosmic ballet.
Whirling dust in the night sky,
Echoes of laughter; watch them fly.

Galaxies swirl with grace divine,
Each twinkle holds a hidden sign.
Mirrored dreams in a starlit trance,
We are but players in this dance.

Comets streak with fleeting glow,
Carving paths where wishes go.
In the space where silence hums,
The heart awakens; adventure drums.

Listen close to the night's refrain,
As magic weaves a soft, sweet chain.
Hold tight your dreams, don't let them fade,
In sparkling echoes, memories are made.

With every heartbeat, time can bend,
In this hush, all sorrows mend.
Join the stars in their timeless chance,
Feel the rhythm of a celestial dance.

Hues of Magic in Hidden Corners

In corners where shadows softly creep,
Tiny miracles begin to leap.
Colors bright in a world so gray,
Whispering secrets of a brighter day.

A sprinkle of dust, a shimmer of light,
Turns the mundane into pure delight.
Through the cracks of reality's door,
Lies a palette of magic to explore.

Vibrant blooms in a garden of dreams,
Reflecting life in delicate seams.
Every petal holds a timeless tale,
In hues of magic, hearts will sail.

A butterfly's flight can mend the soul,
In every moment, we find our role.
So seek the colors, let them unfurl,
In hidden corners of this vast world.

From twilight's brush to dawn's embrace,
Magic lingers in every space.
With each hue, let your spirit roam,
For in life's palette, you'll find your home.

Shimmering Hopes Woven by Celestial Hands

Through cosmic threads, our fates entwine,
In shimmering hopes, where dreams align.
Stars are stitched in the fabric of night,
Guiding our paths with gentle light.

Celestial hands in a dance of grace,
Weaving wisdom into time and space.
Every glimmer, a promise made,
In the tapestry of life, never to fade.

As the dawn breaks with golden hues,
Hope ignites in the morning muse.
We rise anew, with spirits bold,
In shimmering hopes, our stories unfold.

Each heartbeat whispers a silent vow,
To cherish the moment, to live in the now.
With dreams as our guide, and courage as flame,
We journey forth, never the same.

So gather the stardust, let it ignite,
In shimmering hopes, let your heart take flight.
For the universe sings a song so grand,
Woven together by celestial hands.

Enchanted Sails Over Illusory Seas

Upon the waves so blue and bright,
The sails unfurl with whispered light.
With magic winds in secret play,
They dance and glide, then drift away.

Beneath the stars, the dreams we weave,
In moonlit nights, we dare believe.
Each gust a tale yet to be spun,
In twilight's glow, our hearts can run.

The skies embrace a shimmering hue,
With mermaids calling, songs so true.
Their laughter echoes 'neath the tide,
In this vast realm, we laugh and glide.

Yet danger lurks in shadows deep,
For not all whispers promise keep.
A storm may brew, a frown unfurls,
Yet through it all, our hope still twirls.

So set your course, through night's dismay,
With every dawn, we'll find our way.
The stars direct, the sea will tell,
Of enchanted sails and magic well.

The Radiance of Myth Lost in Time

In ages past, when still they soared,
The myths were tales of hearts adored.
With heroes bold and shadows cast,
They whispered truths that seemed to last.

Upon the winds, their stories flew,
Of dragons fierce and lovers true.
In golden fields, the legends bloomed,
Yet shadows grasped, and tales were doomed.

The ancients spoke of shimmering light,
That danced through dark, a beacon bright.
Yet as the years began to wane,
The echoes faded, lost in pain.

What of the lore that shaped our years?
The laughter lost, the hidden tears?
As time stands still, we seek and strive,
To find the spark that keeps them alive.

In every heart, a flicker glows,
Of magic's touch and sacred prose.
For though the ages come and go,
The myths remain, in hearts they grow.

Celestial Bonds in a World of Whimsy

In realms where laughter fills the air,
The stars align with joyous flair.
A tapestry of dreams in flight,
In whimsy's grasp, the world feels right.

With playful sprites on clouds they glide,
Their giggles dance, they do not hide.
They weave and spin with magic thread,
Creating wonders as they tread.

Beneath the moon's delicate gaze,
The night ignites with sparkling blaze.
A carnival of wishes bright,
Where every soul can touch the light.

As shadows play, the colors blend,
In this domain, where rules can bend.
Oh, how celestial bonds will gleam,
In every heart, a vibrant dream!

So let us twirl in joyous cheer,
With laughter loud, we conquer fear.
In a world where whimsy reigns supreme,
Together, we will chase the dream.

Threads of Gold and Silver Dawn

In early light, when shadows fade,
The sun bequeaths a golden braid.
Threads of warmth, entwined with grace,
Awake the day in soft embrace.

Each dewdrop glimmers on the ground,
As whispers call, a hushed surround.
From slumber deep, the world awakes,
With shimmering hues that morning makes.

The silver skies, a canvas bright,
Where dreams are painted in pure light.
A tapestry of hope unspun,
In every heart, the day's begun.

As time unfurls its gentle hand,
We tread along this golden land.
With every step, a tale unfolds,
In threads of silver, bravery bold.

So greet the dawn with open eyes,
For beauty lives in every rise.
In threads of gold, our lives entwined,
A brighter path is yours to find.

The Veil of Dawn on Magical Beasts

In twilight's glow, they softly roam,
With gentle eyes, they find their home.
A dragon's breath, a phoenix's song,
In the dawn's warm light, they all belong.

Threads of magic weave through the air,
Unseen wonders, beyond compare.
The unicorn prances, proud and free,
While griffins soar o'er shadowed trees.

Each wingbeat whispers of ancient lore,
Tales of magic to ever explore.
In secret glades where wild things play,
The veil of dawn steals night away.

As sunbeams dance on misty morn,
A bond is forged, forever sworn.
In the heart of the wild, hope takes flight,
Among the beasts, all is right.

So heed the call of the early light,
For in its warmth, all fears take flight.
Embrace the magic that draws you near,
In the veil of dawn, all hearts appear.

Sunkissed Whispers in Fabled Fields

In fields where sunlight gently spills,
The wind carries whispers, of ancient thrills.
Golden wheat and flowers bright,
Dance together in warm delight.

Beneath the boughs of the old oak tree,
Dreamers gather, hearts set free.
Tales of yore and fables spun,
In every shadow, stories run.

The brook hums soft, its melody sweet,
As fireflies twinkle, with nimble feet.
A tapestry woven with laughter and sighs,
Where time drifts gently, beneath blue skies.

Each petal's flutter, a secret shared,
With every step, a soul laid bare.
The sun dips low, casting gold and green,
In this enchanted, peaceful scene.

So come, dear friend, and wander with me,
In these fabled fields, forever free.
For every whisper holds a tale,
A journey spun like a gentle gale.

A Tapestry of Hope in Fantastical Landscapes

Across the hills where dreams take flight,
In colors bold and pure delight.
The mountains rise, like giants strong,
Guardians of tales that sing along.

Rivers glisten with a silver sheen,
In their depths, echoes of things unseen.
Forests whisper with a haunting grace,
Inviting wanderers to find their place.

Each star above, a guiding light,
Illuminating paths through the night.
In every shadow, a new chance grows,
A tapestry woven with hopes and woes.

The skies, adorned with hues of gold,
Embrace the stories yet untold.
In the gentle sway of breeze and bloom,
Lies the promise of a brightened room.

So let your spirit soar and sing,
In fantastical landscapes, spread your wings.
For every heartbeat, a chance to see,
A world alive with mystery.

Threads of Wonder in a Dreamer's Heart

Within the heart where dreams reside,
Threads of wonder intertwine with pride.
Each fantasy whispers sweet and low,
Filling the soul, with a gentle glow.

Through corridors of the mind so vast,
Where echoes of laughter shape the past.
A tapestry rich with shimmering stars,
Guides the way through night's soft bars.

In secret gardens, a vision grows,
In shimmering dew, the magic flows.
Every flower, a story to share,
In the quiet moments, joys laid bare.

So dare to dream and weave your song,
In a world where all can belong.
For every thread, a tale unfolds,
In a dreamer's heart, where hope beholds.

With each new dawn, let visions start,
Embrace the threads that fill your heart.
In the dance of dreams, life's beauty lies,
For every moment holds the skies.

Echoes of Ancient Legends in Silken Weaves

In the hush of twilight's grace,
Ancient whispers softly trace,
Tales of heroes, proud and bold,
Woven in the fabric of gold.

In shadows where the secrets sleep,
Gentle dreams and promises keep,
Every stitch a story spun,
In the loom where time is done.

Through the tapestry of yore,
Lives entwined, forevermore,
Silken threads that shimmer bright,
Illuminate the velvet night.

A phoenix rising from its ash,
Legends in a fleeting flash,
Echoes dance through air so sweet,
In the tapestry, lives entreat.

With each weave, the past ignites,
Magic stirs in silken sights,
Threads of fate forever bind,
Echoes linger, long defined.

Shimmering Pathways to Splendid Realms

Beneath the stars, a path appears,
A shimmering trail that calms our fears,
With every step, the world unfolds,
A tale of wonders waiting bold.

In twilight's hush, the whispers call,
As moonlight dances, shadows fall,
Glimmering portals spread their wings,
Inviting hearts to touch the springs.

Through fields of stardust, dreams take flight,
Guided by the softest light,
Each twinkle holds a future bright,
In splendid realms, we chase the night.

Through enchanted groves and streams that gleam,
We wander lost in magic's dream,
With every heartbeat, every sigh,
The universe calls, we fly high.

In this mosaic, life reveals,
The shimmering threads of what it feels,
Together we shall dance, embrace,
In splendid realms, we find our place.

Gossamer Clouds of Myth and Wonder

Softly draped in misty veils,
Gossamer clouds weave ancient tales,
Of creatures born in twilight's glow,
And secrets only dreamers know.

In the realm where fantasies lie,
Where wishes whisper, wings will fly,
Each vapor holds a story spun,
Of battles lost and victories won.

The winds of time begin to blow,
Carrying whispers, pure as snow,
Every flake a myth reborn,
In soft embrace of early morn.

With each touch, the skies ignite,
Colors dance in pure delight,
From clouds that cradle hopes anew,
In the light, what dreams can do.

Beneath such skies, our spirits rise,
In gossamer clouds, truth never lies,
With every dreamer, worlds combine,
In wonder's grasp, our hearts align.

Traces of Magic in Starlit Skies

In the silence of the night,
Stars awaken, shining bright,
Every glimmer holds a spark,
Traces of magic in the dark.

With twinkling eyes, the cosmos glows,
In every beat, the universe flows,
Across the heavens, stories soar,
Of ancient magic, forevermore.

In constellations, dreams take flight,
Guided by the silver light,
They tell of journeys, old and new,
Of galaxies where magic brews.

With open hearts, we reach so high,
Seeking whispers from the sky,
In the dance of stars, we find,
The traces left by humankind.

Each glowing orb, a tale unwinds,
Of hopes and dreams and heartbeats kind,
In starlit skies, our spirits soar,
In magic's embrace, forevermore.

Glistening Trails of the Mythic Quest

In shadows deep, where whispers call,
The stars alight, their glimmers small.
With hearts ablaze, we forge ahead,
To seek the truths that others dread.

Through tangled woods, where legends grow,
The path unwinds, a secret flow.
With courage bold and spirits high,
We'll chase the dreams that dare to fly.

The moonlight spills like silver chains,
On every step, our fate remains.
In trials fierce, we find our worth,
A bond unbreakable on this earth.

Each twist and turn, a tale unfolds,
In ancient words, the future holds.
With every heartbeat, time will tell,
The magic lives, our quest so well.

When dawn arrives with golden rays,
We'll stand together, lost in praise.
For every step of this grand quest,
Has woven us, forever blessed.

Enigmatic Weaves of the Seraph's Touch

In twilight's glow, a soft refrain,
The whispers brush like summer rain.
With feathers light, the seraphs sing,
In woven threads, their secrets cling.

The tapestry of night unfurls,
With every stitch, the magic swirls.
In patterns rich, the stories loom,
A dance of fate, in shadows' room.

Through realms unseen, where dreams reside,
We follow paths that love provides.
In every fiber, wisdom flows,
The seraph's gift, in silence grows.

With boundless grace, they weave the skies,
A symphony where hope complies.
In every heart, their echoes hum,
With every beat, we become one.

So let us twine in peace divine,
In mystic realms where starlight shines.
In every breath, their light we clutch,
Embraced forever by their touch.

Celestial Ribbons of the Dawn's Embrace

As dawn breaks forth with tender glee,
The world awakens, wild and free.
In amber hues, the ribbons glide,
With every ray, our hopes abide.

The sky spills secrets, vast and wide,
With whispered dreams, we run and hide.
The morning's breath, a fragrant sigh,
In every glimmer, love draws nigh.

With every heartbeat, light cascades,
In gentle waves, the darkness fades.
Awakening to joys anew,
Each moment paints a brighter hue.

Beneath the arch of sky's embrace,
We find our steps, a sacred space.
In laughter's song, and blessings warm,
We gather strength to weather storm.

So let us dance in dawn's sweet light,
On ribbons spun, our spirits flight.
With every sunrise, dreams take flight,
In unity, behold the sight.

Threaded Peace in Mythic Landscapes

In landscapes rich with time's caress,
Where magic dwells, and hearts confess.
With every step on emerald fields,
A sense of peace the spirit yields.

The mountains tower, proud and grand,
Their ancient wisdom, close at hand.
In every brook, a tale runs free,
Of solace found, beneath the tree.

In whispers soft, the winds will tell,
Of love entwined in nature's spell.
With arms outstretched, we let it flow,
In harmony, our spirits grow.

The sun dips low, in crimson hue,
As twilight wraps the land in blue.
In shadowed glens, paths intertwine,
A tapestry of fate divine.

With every heartbeat, trust will guide,
In mythic lands, we stand beside.
For peace is woven through the strife,
In every thread, the pulse of life.

Celestial Lattice of the Unicorn's Secret

In moonlit glades where secrets dream,
A unicorn weaves a silvery beam.
Its horn aglow with ancient lore,
Unlocks the path to the mystic shore.

Amongst the stars, a dance unfolds,
With whispers soft, the night beholds.
A tapestry of light and grace,
Guiding lost souls through time and space.

With gentle hooves on silken grass,
Each step reveals what shadows amass.
The woven threads of fate align,
In harmony, their fates entwine.

In every heart, a spark ignites,
The magic lies in tender sights.
For those who seek the truths untold,
Shall find the light, their hearts consoled.

Beneath the gaze of twinkling eyes,
Where dreams take flight and never die.
The unicorn stands, a timeless guide,
In the celestial lattice, worlds collide.

Ethereal Glimmers Across the Stardust Fields

Upon the fields where stardust swirls,
Ethereal glimmers paint all the worlds.
With every breeze, the cosmos sighs,
As magic weaves through velvet skies.

The moonlight drapes its silver shawl,
A gentle peace, embracing all.
Each twinkle tells a tale so old,
Of lovers lost and destinies bold.

In whispers low, the night unfolds,
With vibrant dreams and legends told.
The stars align in patterns bright,
Creating paths of pure delight.

Here in the quiet, hearts take flight,
Across the stardust, pure and light.
With hopes and wishes, we ascend,
To seek the places where dreams blend.

As dawn approaches, shadows flee,
The fields awake, forever free.
In every glimmer, truth remains,
As ethereal whispers form our chains.

Fantastical Yarns of Myth and Memory

In tales spun bright with fiery thread,
Fantastical yarns of dreams long dead.
Each memory dances, a fleeting ghost,
In the heart's chamber, they wander most.

From whispered lore of ancient lands,
To forgotten spells in timeless hands.
The echoes linger, both soft and bold,
In the tapestry of life retold.

Through shimmering mists of twilight's grace,
We chase the shadows that time can't erase.
With every heartbeat, a story blooms,
In the silent spaces between our rooms.

The weaver's loom is always near,
With every stitch, the past is clear.
In every thread, a legacy's breath,
In fantastical dreams, we dance 'til death.

As stars unite in the cosmic sea,
The myths revive eternally.
In stories shared and smiles embraced,
The magic lives in time's warm chase.

Radiant Echoes of Celestial Whispers

In quiet nights, when dreams take flight,
Radiant echoes dance in the light.
Celestial whispers call our name,
As stardust weaves a fiery flame.

Each twinkling star, a secret told,
Of cosmic journeys, brave and bold.
Across the heavens, spirits soar,
In luminous tales forevermore.

The moon will guard our tender fears,
As ancient magic draws us near.
With every pulse, our souls entwine,
In radiant echoes, the stars align.

From depths unknown, we lift our gaze,
To chase the light through timeless haze.
Each secret shared, a sacred trust,
In the universe vast, we find our must.

So gather close, let visions reign,
In celestial whispers, love's refrain.
For in the night, our hearts compose,
A symphony where the stardust glows.

Shining Trails through the Realm of Wonder

Beneath the stars, a path unfolds,
Whispers of dreams in silvery gold.
Through forests deep, where secrets dwell,
Adventure calls, a sweet, bold spell.

In glades where fairies twirl and gleam,
There lies a way to every dream.
With laughter high and hearts so light,
We chase the dawn, embracing night.

Mountains rise, their peaks alight,
Guardians of both day and night.
With every step, we learn to see,
The magic bound in you and me.

A river hums a timeless tune,
Under the watchful, whispered moon.
It leads us forth to realms anew,
Where wonders dance and skies are blue.

So journey on, through fields of dreams,
Life's tapestry is more than it seems.
With every breath, feel the embrace,
Of shining trails in this wondrous place.

Weaver of Twilight and Mythic Shadows

In twilight's grasp, the shadows weave,
A tale of magic, we believe.
With threads of silver and whispers low,
A story blooms, where dreams can grow.

Stars whisper secrets in the night,
Guiding us softly, pure delight.
Through hidden paths where shadows sway,
We find the light to lead our way.

The moonlit dance of ancient lore,
Calls us to seek and to explore.
A flicker here, a shimmer there,
In every corner, magic's air.

Embrace the night, let worries flee,
For every shadow hides a key.
Unlock the dreams that softly call,
With gentle grace, we stand so tall.

So let us weave this mystic thread,
In twilight's world, where few have tread.
A tapestry of joy and light,
Forever bound in endless night.

Magical Patterns of the Celestial Dance

Under the sky, where wonders gleam,
Stars unite in a cosmic dream.
Each twinkle tells a story bright,
Of endless realms and quiet flight.

The planets spin in a graceful waltz,
Each movement flows without a fault.
Together they paint the night so fair,
With colors bright, beyond compare.

Galaxies swirl in an astral grace,
Time and space in a warm embrace.
We feel the pull of ancient lore,
As constellations whisper more.

The universe sings a lullaby,
To hearts that wander, dreams that fly.
With every beat, we find our way,
In magical patterns where we stay.

So gaze above, let visions soar,
For in the dance, there's always more.
A tapestry of night divine,
In celestial realms, our spirits shine.

Glittering Ties to the First Light of Dawn

As dawn breaks forth with golden rays,
The world awakens from its haze.
With every shimmer, hope ignites,
In joyful hues, the heart delights.

The morning dew on blades of grass,
Reflects the dreams that come to pass.
With gentle whispers, nature sings,
Of endless joys that daylight brings.

Clouds drift softly, a canvas bright,
Painting stories in morning light.
Each color glows, a promise new,
Of all the wonders yet in view.

So let us chase the sun's ascent,
In its embrace, our spirits lent.
With every step, we find our grace,
In glittering ties to time and space.

As day unfolds, remember well,
The magic found in every tell.
For in the dawn, we truly see,
The world of wonders meant to be.

Glistening Yarns from the Wellspring of Dreams

In the quiet of night, where the shadows dance,
Threads of silver weave their chance.
Each glimmering strand, a tale untold,
Whispers of wonder in the dark so bold.

Of heroes long gone, and places unseen,
Fates entwined like a shimmering sheen.
The tapestry glows with magic's embrace,
Where hopes take flight in a timeless space.

A fabric of starlight, a whisper, a sigh,
Dreams stitched together, soaring high.
In the loom of the night, secrets interlace,
A wondrous adventure in this dreamscape place.

So gather your dreams, let them softly flow,
In the glistening yarns where imaginations grow.
For the wells of creation are endless and deep,
In the realm of our dreams, where we dare to leap.

And when dawn approaches, the magic may fade,
But the threads of the night in our hearts shall stay made,
For every bright spark that has danced in our mind,
Is a piece of our soul that we're destined to find.

Transcendent Strings in Twilight's Play

As twilight descends, the stars start to sing,
A symphony born on the night's gentle wing.
Strings weave through the air, a delicate thread,
Binding all dreams in a twilight spread.

With each note that flutters, the shadows ignite,
Transcendent in beauty, enveloping night.
The echoes of laughter, the whispers of grace,
In the dance of the darkness, the light finds its place.

From the depths of the heavens, the melodies soar,
Bringing forth wonders we yearn to explore.
The sky becomes canvas, as colors unite,
Transcendent strings painting twilight's light.

With every new heartbeat, the world seems to sway,
As magic unfolds in the twilight's array.
Each fleeting moment, a gift to embrace,
In the symphony spun through this luminous space.

So listen, dear heart, to the strings of the night,
For in their soft music, all spirits take flight.
In the twilight's enchantment, dreams come alive,
Together we flourish, together we thrive.

Whispered Wonders from the Fabric of Night

In the hush of the night, secrets begin,
A fabric woven with whispers within.
Each sigh of the stars, a tale softly spun,
A story of wonders, for everyone.

The moon dances lightly, casting its glow,
Over fields of dreams where shadows do flow.
With every faint whisper, a spark is ignited,
In the fabric of night where hope is united.

Soft melodies linger in the cool evening air,
Painting our hearts with a gentle flair.
Whispers entwine through the dark, like a song,
A chorus of magic where we all belong.

The night cradles wishes, each twinkling light,
A promise of dreams that take flight in the night.
From the depths of our souls, let desires unfold,
As the fabric of night wraps us in its fold.

So cherish the whispers, let them inspire,
For in every shadow, there lies a fire.
Whispered wonders beckon us near,
In the stillness of night, casting away fear.

Dazzling Echoes of Fantasia's Embrace

In realms of enchantment, where magic is spun,
Dazzling echoes of dreams brightly run.
Fields filled with laughter, colors that gleam,
Fantasia's embrace holds the heart's fervent dream.

Every heartbeat echoes through valleys and hills,
In the joyful embrace where the spirit fulfills.
Each shimmer and sparkle, a promise of light,
A dance of creation, enchanting the night.

The whispers of fairies in twilight's soft breath,
Call forth the visions that conquer all death.
In the embrace of the night, we are never alone,
For Fantasia's spirit has always been home.

Let go of your fears, let your dreams take their flight,
For dazzling echoes await in the night.
Through the fabric of magic, our stories are spun,
In Fantasia's heart, all our journeys begun.

So gather the memories, weave them with care,
For in those bright echoes, we'll always be there.
In this realm of creation where wonders arise,
Dazzling echoes of dreams dance across the skies.

Celestial Stitches in Dawn's Embrace

In the hush of morning light,
Threads of gold begin to weave,
Stitching dreams in soft delight,
Waking worlds that dare believe.

Misty whispers brush the trees,
As sunlight dances on the dew,
Nature hums in gentle pleas,
To share the magic born anew.

Stars retreat, their secrets kept,
While shadows bow to radiant flare,
In this tapestry, all are swept,
Into the dawn's enchanted care.

Each petal blooms with stories shared,
Unraveling threads of history,
In every heart, a voice declared,
A chorus sweet of mystery.

So let us tread on golden trails,
Where dreams and dawn entwine as one,
In celestial stitches, bright and frail,
Awakening with the rising sun.

Radiant Tales of Gossamer Dreams

Through the night, the whispers weave,
In shadows deep, soft visions hide,
Gossamer threads that we believe,
Capture hope where spirits glide.

Moonlight spills like silver rain,
Over hills and valleys wide,
Each flicker holds a sweet refrain,
A promise where our dreams reside.

Beneath the stars, our fancies soar,
On wings of light, they float and glide,
Every heartbeat, yearning for
A journey where our hearts confide.

In starlit skies, the night unfolds,
Radiant tales in whispers spun,
Of love and courage, brave and bold,
Embracing all beneath the sun.

So dream with me, where visions blend,
In the tapestry of night's sweet gleam,
For in these tales, true magic bends,
Weaving life into our dream.

The Ethereal Weave of Twilight Hues

As twilight drapes its velvet cloak,
The world is stitched in shades of grace,
Each breath a spell, each word bespoke,
In this enchanted, hidden place.

Threads of lavender and fire,
Dance upon the evening's sigh,
An ethereal tale, a burning desire,
Where the dreams and shadows lie.

Whispers caught in the twilight's seam,
Binding fates like stars that gleam,
In every heart, a fragile dream,
Unfurling hopes, a gentle beam.

Amidst the night, we find our thread,
In the quiet hush of dusk's embrace,
Creating art, where none have tread,
Awakening the hidden grace.

So linger here, as day descends,
In twilight hues, our dreams awake,
For in this weave, the night extends,
A promise held in every ache.

Glimmering Fibers in a Mythical Sky

In skies adorned with flecks of light,
Glimmering fibers drift and sway,
A tapestry of wonder bright,
Where tales of old begin to play.

Every star a whispered story,
Every breeze a gentle call,
In cosmic realms, adorned with glory,
Where dreams are stitched to rise and fall.

Beneath the vast, unending show,
The fabric of our hearts align,
In celestial dance, above we go,
Threading hopes through space and time.

With every twinkle, spells are cast,
Creating worlds where we can roam,
Through glimmering threads, forever vast,
In the heart of a mythical home.

So take my hand, let's soar away,
On glimmering fibers, wild and free,
In a sky where dreams can play,
Together, we shall find our sea.

Patches of Light in the Woven Cosmo

In the tapestry where stars collide,
Fleeting shadows dance and glide,
Magic whispers through the night,
Patches of soft, silvery light.

Beneath the gaze of celestial eyes,
Dreamers weave their gentle sighs,
Threads of hope in twilight spun,
Binding hearts, two into one.

Eons passed in stellar flight,
We find solace, take our flight,
For in this vast, enchanted sea,
Every soul is meant to be.

As the cosmos gently hums,
Sweetest melodies encompassed drums,
Within this still, eternal song,
All of us truly belong.

Through galaxies where stardust beams,
Woven worlds ignite our dreams,
Infinite wonders, softly bright,
Patches of light in the woven night.

Enchanted Whispers Through Variegated Skies

Underneath the vast expanse,
Colors blend in a mystic dance,
Whispers float on the gentle breeze,
Guiding hearts like crooked trees.

Each hue reflects a story told,
Of heart's desires and dreams bold,
In scattered twilight, secrets lie,
Enchanted whispers through the sky.

Stars spill laughter, twinkling bright,
Painting wonders with pure delight,
In every sunrise, tales unfold,
In each sunset, memories gold.

Moments flicker like fireflies,
In the shadows where magic lies,
Through a canopy of boundless flight,
Enchanted whispers dance in light.

For in the twilight's gentle call,
We find the spark that binds us all,
Through variegated skies we soar,
In endless dreams forevermore.

Rays of Inspiration through Cosmic Lattice

In the cradle of night's embrace,
We wander through this sacred space,
Rays of brilliance, softly cast,
Piercing through the veil of past.

Threads of wisdom weave their way,
Illuminating night and day,
Each glimmer beckons us to find,
The secrets that the stars have lined.

Cosmic lattice, spun so bright,
Guides the hearts seeking light,
A celestial map, drawn above,
Whispering tales of hope and love.

In the mystery of twinkling glow,
We trace the paths where dreams can flow,
For in each ray, a chance to grow,
Through cosmic lattice, wisdom's flow.

Together we rise, hand in hand,
Across the night, a woven strand,
Rays of inspiration, endless flight,
Through the cosmos, our guiding light.

Sparkling Hyacinths of Mythical Radiance

In gardens lush where legends bloom,
Sparkling hyacinths dispel all gloom,
With colors bright, their stories weave,
Each petal whispers, softly grieve.

In the moonlight's tender touch,
Dreamers find peace, oh, so much,
Glimmers dance on dew's embrace,
Mythical radiance fills the space.

With every breeze, adventures start,
Crafting tales that warm the heart,
From fragile roots arise the bold,
In shimmering hues, secrets unfold.

Together they sing of days gone by,
In every bloom, a silent sigh,
As hope ignites in colors bright,
Sparkling hyacinths, pure delight.

Through gardens lush, love intertwines,
In a tapestry of sacred signs,
Mythical tales, in fragrance rise,
Within these blooms, the truth complies.

Seraphic Threads of Celestial Magic

In the realm where whispers play,
Threads of light in skies of gray.
Stars weave stories, bright and bold,
With secrets of the night retold.

Crafted by the hands of fate,
Each stitch a dream to recreate.
The cosmos hums a lilting tune,
As the moon dances with the sun at noon.

Angelic beings softly glide,
Through the shadows, they will bide.
Every twinkle, a gentle sigh,
Dreams unfurling, soaring high.

In realms unseen, where magic brews,
Colors dance in vibrant hues.
Golden threads and silver strands,
Weaving wonders with delicate hands.

So let us follow this ancient art,
With seraphic threads that spark the heart.
For in this fabric, we'll find our place,
In the embrace of time and space.

Fairy's Loom and Cosmic Dyes

In gardens where the fairies tread,
A loom of dreams is gently spread.
Cosmic dyes in every hue,
Painting worlds both old and new.

With each flicker of a wand,
Threads of fate are deftly fond.
Whispers of the universe call,
As starlight weaves through it all.

Glowing orbs of twilight's grace,
Dance with kindness, soft embrace.
Each woven piece, a tale to share,
Born from hopes, spun from air.

The nightingale sings, a sweet refrain,
As dreamers gather, thoughts untamed.
In this tapestry, dreams unite,
Guiding souls through endless night.

So take a thread, let wonder bloom,
In the fairy's loom, there's endless room.
With cosmic dyes, let spirits soar,
In magic's realm, forevermore.

Prismatic Woven Dreams of Starlight

Beneath the canopy of night,
Prismatic dreams take wondrous flight.
Woven gently with starlit thread,
In the twilight, dreams are bred.

Each glimmer sparkles, softly gleams,
Echoing the heart's own dreams.
A tapestry of hopes and fears,
Stitched with laughter, sewn with tears.

With every wish, a strand appears,
Binding moments through the years.
Celestial whispers share their lore,
In woven dreams, we dare to soar.

The cosmos twirls in midnight grace,
Creating patterns, finding space.
Every stitch a timeless rhyme,
Echoing the beats of love and time.

So close your eyes and feel the weave,
In prismatic light, we shall believe.
For in these dreams, our spirits play,
In starlit realms, we find our way.

Enchanted Ribbons of the Fabled Heart

In twilight's glow, the ribbons sway,
Enchanted whispers lead the way.
Through winding paths and forest deep,
The fabled heart begins to leap.

Each ribbon tells a tale of old,
Of bravery, and love, and gold.
With every twist, a secret spins,
In vibrant colors, magic begins.

As moonlight bathes the earth with dreams,
The air is filled with silver beams.
Feelings woven with tender care,
In every corner, a spark lays bare.

With threads of hope, the heart is bound,
In enchanted realms, where joy is found.
A symphony of love takes flight,
Through ribbons dancing in the night.

So hold these ribbons, let them guide,
Through every joy, and every tide.
For in the weave of fate's own art,
We find our peace in the fabled heart.

Ethereal Beacons in the Forest's Heart

In secret glades where moonbeams dance,
The silver whispers find their chance.
Among the trees of emerald grace,
Ethereal beacons weave their lace.

They shimmer soft through misty air,
Guiding hearts with tender care.
In the quiet, magic sings,
As night unfolds her velvet wings.

Each glow a story, wild and bright,
Glimpses of the hidden light.
In shadows deep, their secrets lie,
Waiting for the brave to try.

The forest breathes a gentle hum,
A symphony of all that's come.
With every step, the spirits play,
Inviting souls to join their sway.

So wander deep where dreams entwine,
And seek the stars in whispers fine.
For in the heart of woods so bold,
Ethereal beacons grace the old.

Tapestry of Wonders in a Waking Dream

In lands where twilight softly drapes,
A tapestry of wonders shapes.
Threads of gold and silver gleam,
Weaving tales from every dream.

Each colored strand a life unfolds,
Of whispered wishes and secrets told.
Through the loom of night and day,
Magic dances, wild and gay.

With every stitch, the stories twine,
A flicker bright from realms divine.
In gardens where the spirits play,
Dreamers gather, lost in sway.

The wonders call with gentle grace,
Inviting hearts to join the chase.
In waking hours of sunlit beams,
We glimpse the truths within our dreams.

So wander forth where shadows gleam,
And lose yourself in every scheme.
For life is but a splendid weave,
A waking dream, so rare to leave.

The Spectral Glow of Enchanted Realms

Beyond the vale where shadows creep,
A spectral glow awakens deep.
In enchanted realms, the night unfolds,
A dance of magic, ancient, bold.

Beneath the stars that shine so bright,
Whispers echo through the night.
In every glimmer, a tale begins,
Of timeless fables and secret sins.

Around the fire, the spirits sing,
Of lost desires and joyful spring.
With every flicker, hopes arise,
Unveiling dreams beneath the skies.

From visions lost, to futures found,
In spectral light, our dreams abound.
We roam the paths where shadows chase,
Embracing wonders, finding grace.

So venture forth with hearts aglow,
Where enchanted realms await your show.
In the spectral light, find your theme,
And join the dance of every dream.

Celestial Lights in the Myths of Old

In dusk's embrace, the heavens twine,
Celestial lights, pure and divine.
Myths of old in starlit ink,
Guide the wanderers on the brink.

Each star a story penned in time,
Of heroes bold and tales that rhyme.
The skies unveil their ancient grace,
As constellations shine and chase.

From shadows cast through midnight skies,
The whispers blend with softborn sighs.
In the glow of comet's flight,
Dreams take wing, igniting night.

The myths arise from ages past,
In celestial charts, forever cast.
With every flicker, legends breathe,
And in their light, we choose to weave.

So look aloft where wonders soar,
And find the light forevermore.
For in the myths of days gone by,
Celestial lights will never die.

Mystical Radiance of Fabled Journeys

In twilight's glow, the lanterns dance,
Guiding souls in a whispered trance.
With every step on cobbled lanes,
The heart unlocks, where magic reigns.

Through ancient woods, where secrets lie,
Beneath the gaze of a starry sky.
Adventurers old and dreams anew,
In stories spun with threads of dew.

The griffin's call, the phoenix' rise,
Echoing tales beneath the skies.
In the hush of night, we dare to tread,
With every word, the past is fed.

A castle stands, its stones aglow,
With mysteries that the winds bestow.
In chambers deep, the echoes play,
Of promise kept, and hopes that stray.

So gather close, and join the quest,
In fables woven, we find our rest.
For in each journey, a spark we find,
The magic lives in heart and mind.

Glistening Fragments of a Dreamer's Tale

In slumber's grasp, where dreams unfurl,
A world of wonder begins to swirl.
With glistening shards of starlit grace,
The veils of night, a friendly space.

Through crystal streams where wishes flow,
The heart finds solace, the spirit's glow.
Each step we take on moonbeam's track,
A tale unfolds, there's no turning back.

Whispers of sprites in the evening air,
Secrets of realms where few would dare.
A tapestry spun with silver thread,
Of fantasies lived and paths once tread.

In the glow of dawn's soft embrace,
The echoes linger, time can't erase.
So dreamers rise, with courage bold,
In glistening fragments, our tales are told.

Each fleeting moment, a treasure rare,
The magic lies in the dreams we share.
For life is but a wondrous flight,
In every heart, a spark of light.

Translucent Shadows of Enchanted Stories

In the moonlight's sheen, shadows play,
Whispers of tales that drift away.
Translucent forms of lore unfold,
In twilight's arms, the brave and bold.

Beneath the boughs where spirits dwell,
Chasing echoes of a whispered spell.
In every rustle, a story stirs,
Of fleeting moments, and distant whirs.

A flicker, a glimpse of legends past,
The breath of magic, a die is cast.
With every heartbeat, the shadows weave,
An enchanted dance, we dare believe.

Through corridors of time we stride,
In translucent shades, the worlds collide.
Each step we take, a spark ignites,
The shadows guide through enchanted nights.

So gather 'round, take heed and share,
The tales of old, the dreams laid bare.
For in the fading light's gentle glow,
Translucent shadows begin to grow.

Threads of Time in Celestial Patterns

In the fabric of night, where starlight glows,
Threads of time through the cosmos flows.
In patterns woven, each tale aligns,
A dance of ages, in bright designs.

From ancient realms, the whispers rise,
Threads of fate beneath endless skies.
In the loom of dreams, we spin our threads,
With every heartbeat, adventure spreads.

Celestial maps, where wonders meld,
And secrets of time can be unveiled.
Through constellations, our spirits soar,
In patterns woven, forevermore.

So seek the light in the darkest hour,
In threads of fate, we find our power.
Each stitch a moment, each knot a spark,
In the tapestry woven, we leave our mark.

With every journey, the patterns shift,
In the cosmic dance, a timeless gift.
So gather closely, and weave your dreams,
In threads of time, let your spirit gleam.

Threads of Splendor in the Weaver's Embrace

In twilight's glow, a tapestry shines,
With colors bright, where magic entwines.
Each thread a tale, a whispering song,
In the weaver's hands, we all belong.

Patterns emerge from shadows long,
In the loom's dance, the heart grows strong.
With each flicker, a dream takes flight,
In this embrace, we chase the light.

The golden strands of hope and fear,
Weaving together the tales we hear.
In silken threads, the stories trace,
A world alive in the weaver's grace.

Beneath the stars, the fabric flows,
In every stitch, a secret grows.
Each knot a promise, each fold a dream,
In the weaver's art, we all redeem.

So take these threads and hold them tight,
For in our hands, they shine so bright.
With love and care, let's weave anew,
In the splendor of this dance, we're true.

Woven Mysteries of the Spellbound Night

In the hush of night, the stars align,
A tapestry woven with secrets divine.
Moonlit threads, in the cool night air,
Whisper of magic everywhere.

The shadows sway in a rhythmic trance,
Weaving mysteries in a celestial dance.
With every twinkle, a story unfolds,
Of ancient magicians and heroes bold.

Crimson threads of love and despair,
In the fabric of dreams, we all share.
With each pull, the heart's light grows,
In the night's embrace, the wonder flows.

The starlit sky holds tales untold,
Crafted from stardust, both brave and bold.
In woven whispers beneath the moon,
We find our magic, our hearts in tune.

So let the night wrap you in grace,
A tapestry spun in a sacred place.
For in the woven mysteries bright,
We discover ourselves in the spellbound night.

Nebulae Weavings of Joy and Radiance

In cosmic threads that twirl and spin,
Amidst the stars, where dreams begin.
Nebulae glowing with colors rare,
Weaving moments of joy in the air.

Galaxies dance in a cosmic embrace,
Weaving happiness, a sacred space.
Each shimmering light tells tales of old,
Of love's warm embrace and courage bold.

Across the cosmos, the joy expands,
With radiant filaments in our hands.
The night sky's canvas, a brilliant display,
Where joy and light guide our way.

So reach for the stars, let your heart soar,
In nebulae weavings, we find so much more.
Embrace the beauty of what lies above,
In the fabric of the universe, sew your love.

With every spark, find brilliance anew,
In the cosmic dance, let joy ensue.
For in the weavings of joy and light,
We become the magic that fuels the night.

Fantastic Filaments of the Starlit Serenade

Beneath the sky, where stardust swirls,
Fantastic filaments weave and twirl.
Each note a shimmer, each chord a glow,
In the starlit serenade, our hearts flow.

With every strum, the night ignites,
Creating magic, in endless flights.
The music dances through the trees,
Carried away on the gentle breeze.

Woven songs, both tender and grand,
Connecting us all, hand in hand.
With melodies soft, and harmonies bright,
In this serenade, we take to flight.

So let the stars guide your way home,
In the filaments, no need to roam.
For in the magic of this night's embrace,
We find our dreams, in starlit grace.

With every note, let joy arise,
As we sing beneath these endless skies.
For in the fabric of love and song,
We weave together, where we belong.

Mystical Fibers of the Enchanted Realm

In whispers of twilight, secrets unfold,
Threads spun from magic, stories untold.
Dancing in shadows, the fairies rejoice,
Their laughter like wind, a jubilant voice.

Through glades where the starlight caresses the dew,
Patterns emerge, vibrant, in colors so true.
They weave through the night, a luminous trail,
Each fiber a promise, in air they set sail.

Beneath ancient canopies, roots intertwine,
Mystical pathways where realms align.
Every step whispers of fables so bold,
In the heart of the forest, the stories unfold.

The rivers hum softly, a tune to the ground,
As echoes of magic in currents abound.
From trees clad in silver, to stars glowing bright,
Each moment enchanted, a breathtaking sight.

And as dawn breaks the silence, a shimmering hue,
The fibers of magic awaken anew.
With colors that flourish, alive they will thrive,
In the mystical realm, where all dreams arrive.

Illuminated Patterns of Wonder and Delight

In the heart of the evening where wishes escape,
Delightful designs in the starlight take shape.
A canvas of dreams, brushed soft by the night,
Where shadows and moonbeams unite to ignite.

With whims of the wind, they twist and they turn,
Patterns of wonder, like candles, they burn.
Each flicker a glimmer, a promise unspoken,
In the realms of enchantment, no heart shall be broken.

Across fields of forget-me-nots, fragrant and bright,
The tapestry deepens, woven in light.
With threads of ethereal, colors entwined,
Visions of beauty that dance through the mind.

From blossoms that shimmer with dew-dappled grace,
To echoes of laughter in this magical space.
The patterns will whisper, a language divine,
In twinkling reflections, our fates intertwine.

As moonbeams serenade the stillness within,
Illuminated patterns ignite a new spin.
With hearts open wide, let our spirits take flight,
In wonderous splendor, we bask in the night.

Aurora Weaves of Unicorn's Fortune

Where dawn paints the sky with a palette of dreams,
In mystical fabrics, the unicorn gleams.
With feathers of rainbows and whispers of grace,
They gather the twilight to share in the space.

A luminous thread, like a comet in flight,
Weaves through the air, igniting the night.
Their hooves leave a sparkle on paths made of lore,
In the weave of the cosmos, where magic can soar.

Each flick of the mane sends a shiver of awe,
Crafting the stories of legends we saw.
Through valleys of wonder, they gallop with pride,
With golden spun fibers, their fortunes reside.

In twilight's embrace, where moonbeams collide,
The mystery deepens, like waves of the tide.
With colors that shimmer, like stars in the sea,
The aura surrounds us, enchanting and free.

As we chase the horizon, our dreams on a quest,
The unicorn's fortune guides us, a test.
In the glow of auroras, let our spirits fly,
For magic awaits us, where hopes never die.

Brilliant Veins of Otherworldly Glow

In caverns of twilight, where shadows conspire,
Brilliant veins pulse with a shimmering fire.
Threads of pure starlight, like rivers that gleam,
Flow softly through darkness, igniting each dream.

Awake in the silence, where majesty lies,
The essence of worlds flows beneath starry skies.
Each heartbeat a chorus, a symphony rare,
Resonating secrets, in soft whispers' care.

Through labyrinths ancient, where echoes rejoice,
Every breath marks a tale, a mystical voice.
With wonders unfolding, the night gently sways,
In the garden of dreams, where the heart always stays.

As lanterns of twilight illuminate paths,
Veins of creation weave stories that last.
In the dance of the ether, we find our own tune,
Guided by brilliance beneath the soft moon.

So listen and wander, let your spirit flow,
Through realms rich with magic, where time ceases to
know.
For in the depths of the night, let your wonders ignite,
In brilliant veins glowing, you'll find your true light.

Dawn's Glimmer upon Woven Dreams

In the hush of morn, soft light unfurls,
A tapestry bright with the dawn's new pearls.
Whispers of hope in the gentle mist,
Woven with magic, a lover's tryst.

Colors awaken, the shadows retreat,
Beneath the embrace of the sun's warm seat.
Every stitch sings of stories untold,
As daylight dances in threads made of gold.

A gentle breeze stirs memories lost,
In the fabric of dreams, we pay the cost.
Each glimmering bead, each twinkle of light,
Threads of our wishes ignite in the night.

Looms of the past weave the future's design,
In the heart of the dawn, the stars realign.
With each breath we take, new journeys begin,
As dawn's gentle kiss wraps us soft within.

So let your dreams soar upon wings of fate,
In the dawning glow, discover, create.
For within every dawn, hope's brilliance gleams,
As we follow the whispers of woven dreams.

Silken Echoes of the Unicorn's Wish

In the glade where magic twines with the trees,
Silken echoes float on a gentle breeze.
A unicorn's wish, pure as winter's snow,
In the hush of the night, softly whispers low.

Moonlight weaves spells through the leaves overhead,
Painting silver dreams where the gentle hooves tread.
Each flick of its mane sets the starlight ablaze,
In the heart of the forest, lost in a haze.

From the depths of the woods, secrets arise,
As the unicorn dances 'neath the vast, sky-wide eyes.
Hope springs eternal in the twilight hue,
Crafting magic anew, as the night bids adieu.

With each silken step, it beckons us near,
To believe in the dreams that dissolve our fear.
So close your eyes tight, let your spirit take flight,
In the echoes of wishes, bask in the light.

For in every heart rests a silken desire,
To chase the elusive, to reach ever higher.
Ride the wave of dreams, let the magic unfurl,
In the embrace of the night, let adventure whirl.

Echoing Whispers in the Loom of the Universe

In the silence between every heartbeat's echo,
Lies a tapestry grand, where we all will flow.
Stars whisper secrets, realms intertwined,
In the loom of the universe, all love is aligned.

Galaxies spin with a rhythm divine,
Time dances by, like a waltz so fine.
Each twinkling light tells a story profound,
In the hush of eternity, magic is found.

With each fleeting moment, a thread slips away,
Yet woven together, they long to stay.
Fate's delicate fingers pluck at the strands,
Guiding our souls with invisible hands.

So listen closely to the whispers in night,
For in every shadow, there dances a light.
Loom of the cosmos, vast and so grand,
Holds the secrets of all; our hearts understand.

In this intricate web where our dreams are spun,
We find our connections, where we are one.
With every wish cast upon stardust's flight,
In the loom of the universe, all is made right.

Twilight Threads Beneath Magical Stars

As twilight descends, a soft veil is cast,
Threads of gold shimmer, memories vast.
Beneath the bright stars, our dreams intertwine,
In the fabric of night, every heart is a sign.

The whispering winds carry tales of the light,
As shadows embrace the encroaching night.
Each thread a story yet to be spun,
In the magical dance where the day meets the sun.

With starlit designs painting sky with grace,
We weave our desires in this timeless space.
Twilight threads glimmer, weaving hopes anew,
As the universe beckons, inviting us through.

In each gentle rustle, in every soft sigh,
Lies the promise of dreams waiting to fly.
On the canvas of dusk, our wishes released,
As we gather the magic, our souls are increased.

So cherish the twilight, when dreams softly start,
In the embrace of the night, find peace in your heart.
For beneath all the stars, where our spirits roam free,
Lie the twilight threads of our grand destiny.

Glistening Threads of Fantasy's Embrace

In the heart of the night, where dreams softly weave,
Glistening threads hang, in silver they cleave.
With whispers of magic, and songs of the fey,
Every lost hope finds its shimmering way.

Through trails of stardust, where wishes ignite,
Adventures unfold in the softest of light.
Each heartbeat a tale, each breath a new start,
In the tapestry spun from the depths of the heart.

Beneath ancient trees, where the shadows play games,
Lies a world full of wonder, where nothing's the same.
With secrets of ages stitched into the seams,
We wander through realms crafted from our dreams.

In laughter and sorrow, through whispers we tread,
Glistening visions hold us, where none dare to tread.
Each thread forms a bond, so delicate yet strong,
Embraced by the magic that moves us along.

So let us entwine, as the night softly glows,
In this haven of fantasy, where all love grows.
With hearts open wide, we shall dance and we sing,
To the rhythm of life and the joy that it brings.

Vivid Filaments in Twilight's Caress

As twilight descends, the world stirs awake,
Vivid filaments glow, and the stars softly shake.
With laughter interwoven through whispers of night,
Each thread a connection, a spark burning bright.

The dusk holds its breath, as the shadows dance near,
In the shimmer of darkness, all magic is clear.
With colors that swirl in a kaleidoscope,
We find paths of wonder, and weave them with hope.

By the light of the moon, with its silver embrace,
Vivid stories unfold in this enchanted place.
Where time takes a pause, and the past meets the now,
In the threads of our journeys, we learn to allow.

Breathless, we twirl through the realms yet unroamed,
In twilight's caress, we no longer feel alone.
Each filament glistens, a promise anew,
In the fabric of dreams, we find moments so true.

So follow the pathways that beckon so sweet,
Where vivid filaments guide us with ease.
In the depths of our hearts, the adventure begins,
With courage and joy, every loss turns to wins.

Dazzling Pathways through the Starry Veil

In the stillness of night, 'neath the twinkle of stars,
Dazzling pathways beckon, with stories from afar.
Each constellation whispers of journeys untold,
As we follow their light, through the mystery bold.

The galaxies glimmer, like jewels in a crown,
With secrets of ages, and wonders renowned.
Through nebulous dreams, we are destined to fly,
On the wings of the cosmos, no limits apply.

In this vastness divine, we lose and we find,
The heart of the universe, wondrously kind.
Awash in the brilliance of infinite grace,
We trace dazzling pathways, in time and in space.

With each step we take, 'neath this starry expanse,
The universe dances, inviting our dance.
In the depths of the night, with stars as our guide,
We soar through the realms where our dreams can abide.

So let's not forget, in our quest for the light,
Dazzling pathways linger, to lead us through night.
In the quiet of wonder, we'll gather and share,
The magic within us, a treasure so rare.

Glowing Strands of Imagination's Flight

With each flicker of thought, glowing strands weave and twine,
Imagination takes wing, on a course so divine.
Through valleys of fancy, over mountains of dream,
We navigate freely, with heart's gentle gleam.

These strands pulsate brightly, alive with new tales,
Each vision igniting, as the heart gently sails.
In the realm of the mind, where possibilities bloom,
We wander through gardens that banish all gloom.

Let colors collide in a burst of delight,
As glowing strands guide us through the depth of the night.
Each moment a canvas, where wonder takes flight,
Painting pictures of joy, under moon's silvery light.

In laughter and silence, in colors so pure,
The beauty of thought creates a lasting allure.
With glowing strands leading, we're never alone,
In the core of creation, our spirits have grown.

So take up your dreams, let your imagination soar,
With glowing strands weaving tales forevermore.
In this enchanting dance, we find our truest selves,
As the magic unfolds from the vibrant soul's shelves.

Radiant Weavings of Dreamscapes

In twilight's gentle, whispering grace,
Dreams unfurl in a soft embrace.
Threads of silver and hues of gold,
Stories of wonders whispered and told.

Across the canvas, stars align,
Catch the shimmer of fate's design.
A flicker of hope in the night's cool air,
Illuminated wishes float everywhere.

Mirrored visions dance in the sky,
As wishes and shadows gently fly.
Mosaic fragments of hearts entwined,
In the secret gardens of the mind.

Riddles woven with gossamer thread,
Voices of ancients softly said.
With every heartbeat, a tale anew,
In the realm of dreams, so vivid and true.

So let your spirit take to the winds,
Where the journey of laughter and magic begins.
In radiant weavings, may you find your way,
To the boundless horizons of night and day.

Celestial Fabrics of Mythical Whispers

In the heavens high, the stars alight,
Fables of old call forth the night.
With threads of time and secrets spun,
The moonlight dances, a playful run.

Each whisper carries a timeless song,
Where dreams of the brave and bold belong.
Brush-strokes of starlight paint the air,
Celestial fabrics woven with care.

A tapestry of heartbeats, soft and sweet,
Legends rise as shadows retreat.
Mystical creatures in silence gleam,
Bathed in the colors of twilight's dream.

Fables flourish in the quiet night,
Guided by the shimmering light.
The universe breathes, a cosmic bliss,
In mythical whispers, a lover's kiss.

Among the stars, where wishes ignite,
The fabric of fate shrouded in light.
Embrace the cosmic, let spirits soar,
In the celestial weavings, forevermore.

Shimmering Strands of Enchantment

In the heart of woods, where magic lies,
Shimmering strands catch the starlit skies.
Silken threads weave stories bright,
Illusions dance in the soft, pale light.

Glimmers of wonder ignite the day,
As shadows and marvels weave and sway.
Eager whispers float on the breeze,
Entwined in secrets of ancient trees.

A kaleidoscope of colors unveils,
Adventures await where imagination sails.
With every breath, enchantment grows,
In the garden of dreams, where magic flows.

Cascading laughter rides the moon's beam,
Echoing softly, a shared, hidden dream.
In the quiet, a symphony sings,
Of shimmering strands and mystical things.

So wander freely, let your heart sway,
In realms of enchantment, come what may.
For in each shimmer, a story will start,
Threads of wonders woven in every heart.

Ethereal Tapestry in Moonlit Meadows

In moonlit meadows, where shadows play,
An ethereal tapestry takes the day.
Stars like flowers bloom and shine,
Weaving magic in every line.

Gentle breezes carry sweet sighs,
As the night unveils its starry ties.
Each blade of grass holds tales untold,
In the soft embrace of the night's fold.

Secrets flutter like butterflies bright,
Wrapped in whispers, shimmering light.
With each heartbeat, the night takes wing,
An enchanting symphony of everything.

Wander through dreams where echoes blend,
In moonlit meadows, where spirits mend.
The universe dances, wild and free,
In the hush of night, pure harmony.

So let this night be your guiding star,
In the tapestry of dreams, near and far.
Ethereal whispers await your call,
In the heart of the meadow, magic for all.

Radiant Fabrics of Timeless Stories

In the loom of ages past, tales entwine,
Whispers of magic in every line.
Heroes and dreams, they dance in the light,
Stitched with the moon and woven with night.

Fables of courage in shadows of old,
Fires that flicker with secrets untold.
The fabric of legends, both tattered and whole,
Wraps around hearts and comforts the soul.

Each stitch a memory, each thread a wish,
Bound by the heart, a shimmering fisch.
Happily ever afters echo and sway,
In the radiant fabrics where stories play.

Veils of enchantment, patterns of fate,
Daring to weave the love that awaits.
Songs of the ancients, the dreams we revere,
Thrive in the realms where all things are near.

Times may change, yet the stories remain,
Casting their spell like a gentle rain.
Together we're stitched, in the quilt of the stars,
Radiant fabrics, erasing the scars.

Tapestries of Light Spun from Moonbeams

Moonlit threads in the quiet night,
Crafting the dreams that take their flight.
Weaving the magic with whispers so rare,
Tapestries shimmer in the cool evening air.

Glowing with stories of stars up above,
Embroidered with laughter, hope, and love.
Every twinkle, a tale that is spun,
Layer upon layer, the night has begun.

Fairies and shadows together they dance,
Step into the fabric, take a chance.
Soft colors blend in a shimmering swirl,
The magic in moonbeams begins to unfurl.

Through the delicate strands, the wonders do flow,
Illuminating paths where dreams gently grow.
In this enchanted embrace, let your heart beam,
Find solace and light in the woven moonbeam.

Boundless and bright, like the dawn of the day,
These tapestries guide us along the way.
So take a deep breath, let your spirit ignite,
In the tapestries of light spun from the night.

Glows of Wonder in the Weft of Dreams

In the weft of dreams, where the magic resides,
Glows of wonder in soft, twinkling tides.
The fabric of night drapes softly around,
Whispers of starlight, enchantment profound.

Every pattern a wish, every shimmer a sigh,
Colors that dance in the blink of an eye.
Beneath silver skies, the heart learns to soar,
Wrapped in the comfort of tales evermore.

Through valleys of slumber, the fantasies weave,
Threads made of hope, like webs we believe.
Journeying forward, past shadows and seams,
Revealing the truth in the fabric of dreams.

Brushing the canvas with laughter and tears,
The tapestry breathes through the fabric of years.
With glows of wonder to light up the night,
We're bound by the dreams that take all their flight.

In the quietest moments, the whispers unfold,
Stories untold in the fibers we hold.
In the weft of dreams, where all hearts are sewn,
The glows of our wishes are endlessly known.

Threads of Fantasy Along Enchanted Trails

On enchanted trails where the wildflowers grow,
Threads of fantasy dance in the glow.
Woven with courage, adventure, and cheer,
Carried by whispers of those we hold dear.

The paths that we wander are laced with our dreams,
Magic abounds in the moon's silver beams.
With every footfall, a story unfolds,
In threads of soft colors, the heart gently holds.

Ribbons of starlight adorn the night skies,
Crafting a haven where imagination flies.
Through forests enchanted and rivers that sing,
Threads of our fantasy take to the wing.

With each gentle breeze, let the magic prevail,
Listen for secrets along the soft trail.
The art of the journey is woven quite grand,
In the threads of our fantasies, hand in hand.

So gather your dreams and set forth on this quest,
With threads of adventure, we're truly blessed.
Together we'll wander, in this tale we unveil,
Along the bright path, where no heart will fail.

Whispers of Light in a Unicorn's Nest

In the grove where dreams do dwell,
A unicorn weaves a magic spell.
Silken whispers in the air,
Softly dance without a care.

Moonlit glimmers on silver leaves,
Where every heart a secret weaves.
Gentle breezes brush the night,
With echoes of the fading light.

Stars awaken from their sleep,
Guarding wishes, brave and deep.
In their glow, fair spirits rise,
To paint the dawn across the skies.

Pastel colors, bright and rare,
Bloom with tales beyond compare.
Each petal kissed by dreams anew,
In every shade, a world breaks through.

With laughter wrapped in velvet grace,
They weave together time and space.
In this nest where wonders twine,
The heart shall find its wings to shine.

Threads of Stardust and Enchantment

Starlit threads are sewn tonight,
In the tapestry of delight.
Each glimmer sings a tale untold,
Of ancient lore and spirits bold.

In corners where the shadows weave,
Echoes dance, and dreams believe.
Through whispers soft, the magic flows,
Beneath the moon, the garden glows.

A hint of lavender in the breeze,
Lifts the heart, as time does freeze.
With each shimmer, wishes soar,
In the night, forevermore.

Threads of hope, a shining seam,
Starlight woven in a dream.
In every fiber, a spark of fate,
Which beckons dreams beneath the gate.

With each step upon the ground,
An echo of enchantment found.
In whispered lore of stardust spun,
The journey beckons; it has begun.

Dappled Dreams in a Brighter Realm

In the glen where shadows play,
Dappled dreams find their way.
Sunbeams burst through emerald leaves,
Whispering secrets the heart believes.

Among the flowers, vibrant and wild,
Nature's magic, sweetly crafted and styled.
Softly glowing, the petals gleam,
A world alive with every dream.

Laughter blooms amidst the trees,
Carried gently by the breeze.
With every flutter, a spirit sings,
Of joyous days and wondrous things.

The sun melts into twilight's arms,
Revealing all of nature's charms.
Stars arise in a painted sky,
To guide the heart as it flies high.

A realm of whispers, light, and song,
Where every moment feels so strong.
In dappled hues and gentle grace,
We find a dream, a whispered place.

The Glow of Fantasy's Tapestry

In the heart of the enchanted night,
Fantasy glows with pure delight.
Threads of moonlight softly weave,
A tapestry of dreams to believe.

Colors blend in swirls and bends,
Where magic lingers and never ends.
With every stitch, a story flows,
In every hue, the wonder grows.

Beneath the stars, the visions spark,
Illuminating every hidden mark.
In shadows bright where fairies roam,
The glow of wonder feels like home.

Voices echo through the night,
Casting dreams in silver light.
A dance of shadows, soft and free,
Where every moment holds the key.

The tapestry of dreams unfolds,
A myriad of tales it holds.
With each heart, a thread is spun,
In the glow of fantasy begun.

Woven Whispers from Beyond the Veil

In twilight's hush, a whisper calls,
From shadowed realms where silence sprawls.
Through ancient trees, the secrets weave,
A tapestry where none believe.

The moonlit path, a guide so bright,
Leads souls who wander through the night.
With every breath, the stories sing,
Of lost desires that shadows bring.

Echoes dance on the misty air,
Dreams unspooled from heart's despair.
In the stillness, wisdom rests,
In woven whispers, truth invests.

A flicker here, a shimmer there,
Haunting notes, as if to share.
The veil grows thin, the world awakes,
In whispered words, the heart partakes.

Embrace the lore of days long past,
In every tale, a spell is cast.
Across the realms, the echoes roam,
In woven whispers, we find home.

Celestial Beacons of Fantastical Realms

Within the night, stars brightly gleam,
Each spark a tale, a vibrant dream.
From distant worlds, their stories flow,
Celestial beacons in cosmic glow.

The moon, a sage, with wisdom old,
Holds secrets of the brave and bold.
Through shimmering paths, our fates entwine,
In fantastical realms, we dare to shine.

A silver brook sings to the skies,
Murmuring truths that never die.
Reflected hopes in waters clear,
Echo the dreams we hold most dear.

Beneath the arch of endless night,
Galaxies swirl, a wondrous sight.
Each heartbeat counts, a starlit throng,
In harmony, we all belong.

With every glance at the vast expanse,
We find the magic in each chance.
In celestial whispers, hearts will soar,
To realms uncharted, forevermore.

Glimmering Lattices of Imagination's Birth

In woven dreams, the mind unfolds,
A dance of thoughts, a tale retold.
Glimmering lattices softly sway,
Where visions beckon, night and day.

Each thread a spark, a story spun,
In twilight's glow, our fears are done.
Through realms unseen, our spirits fly,
On wings of hope, we touch the sky.

In each heart's pulse, enchantments glow,
Whispers of magic, depths we know.
A gentle thread connects us all,
In imagination, hear the call.

With every bubble that brightly bursts,
A wild idea, a dream rehearsed.
In lattices bright, we'll find our way,
Painting the night with hues of play.

Address the muse, let language flow,
In every chance, let wonder grow.
Glimmering lattices of delight,
In our dreams, the world ignites.

Threads of Light in Soaring Fantasies

In realms of wonder where shadows drift,
Threads of light weave a precious gift.
Soaring high on the winds of fate,
In whispered hopes, we hesitate.

The dawn unfurls with golden rays,
Illuminating our secret ways.
With every heartbeat, dreams take flight,
In soaring fantasies kissed by light.

Across the skies, the colors blend,
Each hue a promise, a time to mend.
Tales forgotten, now freshly told,
In threads of light, we break the mold.

Embrace the visions, uncoil the thread,
Each shimmering strand, where fears are shed.
Through labyrinths of starlit night,
We chase the magic, hearts alight.

With open arms, let wonder rise,
In every moment, a sweet surprise.
Threads of light in dreams we weave,
In soaring fantasies, we believe.

www.ingramcontent.com/pod-product-compliance
Ingram Content Group UK Ltd.
Pitfield, Milton Keynes, MK11 3LW, UK
UKHW021634200125
4187UKWH00003B/133